# DUET

in A major, K.331

for Two Violins *

**VIOLIN II**

WOLFGANG AMADEUS MOZART
(1756-1791)

MINUETTO.
Allegro moderato.

D.C. al Fine.

# ALLA TURCA.

# DUET

in A major, K. 331
for Two Violins *

## VIOLIN I

WOLFGANG AMADEUS MOZART
(1756-1791)

**MINUETTO.**
Allegro moderato.

**ALLA TURCA.**
Allegro.

VIOLIN I